INDIANS
of the
WOODLAND

INDIANS
of the
WOODLAND
Before and After the Pilgrims

By Beatrice Siegel

Illustrated by
Baptiste Bayhylle Shunatona, Jr.

Walker and Company
New York

First published in the United States of America in 1972 by the Walker
Publishing Company, Inc.

Published simultaneously in Canada by Fitzhenry & Whiteside, Limited,
Toronto.

Trade ISBN: 0-8027-6107-0
Reinforced ISBN: 0-8027-6108-9

Library of Congress Catalog Card Number: 74-186176

Printed in the United States of America

To Sam

Contents

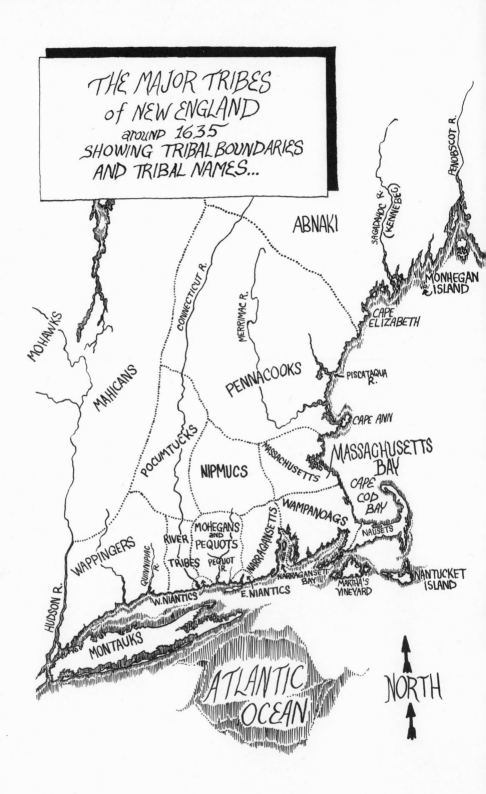

THE MAJOR TRIBES
of NEW ENGLAND
around 1635
SHOWING TRIBAL BOUNDARIES
AND TRIBAL NAMES...

ABNAKI

SAGADAHOC R. (KENNEBEC)

PENOBSCOT R.

MONHEGAN ISLAND

CAPE ELIZABETH

CONNECTICUT R.

MERRIMAC R.

PISCATAQUA R.

MOHAWKS

MAHICANS

PENNACOOKS

CAPE ANN

MASSACHUSETTS

MASSACHUSETTS BAY

POCUMTUCKS

NIPMUCS

CAPE COD BAY

WAMPANOAGS

NAUSETS

MOHEGANS
AND
PEQUOTS

RIVER
TRIBES

WAPPINGERS

QUINNIPIAC R.

PEQUOT IR.

NARRAGANSETTS

NANTUCKET ISLAND

HUDSON R.

W. NIANTICS

E. NIANTICS

NARRAGANSETT BAY

MARTHA'S VINEYARD

MONTAUKS

ATLANTIC OCEAN

NORTH

Who Were the Woodland Indians?

THEY WERE TRIBES OF INDIANS who lived a long time ago in the dense forests that covered eastern America. They lived there long before Columbus discovered America.

The forests at that time stretched along the Atlantic coast from Canada to Florida. They covered mountain and valley. They grew down to the ocean's edge.

Scattered throughout these deep forests were lakes and rivers. Near them Indians cleared the land and built their villages. Everywhere they were surrounded by tall thick trees of birch, pine, oak, ash, elm, chestnut, maple, and cedar. There were nut trees, fruit trees, tangled vines, and tall wild marsh grasses.

The land was fragrant with blossoms and the thick forests were alive with animals and birds. In spring and summer fish filled lakes and streams. Wild fowl made homes in creeks and swamps.

11

Living in the deep forests of what is now known as New England were about 30,000 Woodland Indians. They were divided into six large tribes and many smaller ones. All of them were part of the Algonquian family of Indians. They descended from the same ancestors and they spoke a variation of the Algonquian language.

What kind of people made these forests their homes? How did they get their food? How did they dress? What did children do?

This book tells how the New England tribes lived before the Pilgrims settled in Plymouth in 1620. It tells how they used plants and animals for food, clothes, and housing. It tells about their families and what they did to relax and have fun. You will also learn what happened to these Woodland tribes after the white man settled on their land.

Could you live in the woodlands? Perhaps. If you were an Indian and were brought up to know your sur-

roundings as you know your ABCs, then you would be able to. This book will help you understand the way the Indians lived.

Why do we want to know about them?

As the first Americans, the Indians helped the new Americans settle here. In many ways they helped this country grow.

From their villages along the coast, the Woodland Indians saw the white men land.

The Pilgrims landed in December, 1620. They did not know how to live through the freezing winter. Many died from hunger and sickness. The Woodland Indians helped the others survive the first starving years.

They let the Pilgrims live on their land.

They gave them food.

They taught them how to plant corn, fertilize the soil, and make maple sugar from the maple tree.

They taught them how to build canoes, hunt animals, find plants to eat and plants to cure sickness.

They became guides for explorers. They were fur trappers for traders.

Their narrow winding trails became routes, then roads.

The Woodland Indians *knew* how to live in the wilderness. Their knowledge and skills and assistance made it possible for Europeans to settle in a strange new world.

How Did They Look?

ALMOST EVERYONE HAS SEEN A PICTURE of an Indian. Perhaps you have seen an Indian in a book or in the movies. Perhaps you have even seen a picture of an Indian standing tall and slim and straight aiming his bow and arrow up into the sky. This is the Indian of the eastern woodlands.

Woodland Indians were tall. They looked strong and healthy. They had strong, straight legs, small waists,

and broad shoulders. Their eyes were dark brown and their hair was black and straight.

When young girls combed their hair each day with a wood or bone comb, they rubbed bear fat into it to make it look glossy. They wore it tied back or in braids over each shoulder.

Men had little or no hair on their faces and bodies. They plucked out any they found.

Men often wore their long hair hanging down over their shoulders. Or they cut their hair in any way they wanted to. Usually they shaved off the hair on both sides of their head. They let the center section of hair grow high and hang down their back in a twist or braid.

Their red-brown skin always glistened with whale oil, beaver or bear fat. They rubbed oils into their skin all the time. It protected them against nasty weather, insects, hot sun, and freezing cold.

Often you saw them with painted faces and bodies.

Why did they paint their faces and bodies?

They used paints in ceremonials and wars. Men going to war streaked their faces with red, black, white, and yellow paints. They looked fierce to frighten the enemy.

Paints could tell you how a man felt. When someone died in the family, Indians painted their faces black to show their grief. A man looked sad in mulberry red. He looked cheerful in a bright red band across his forehead.

They used paints as cosmetics to look attractive and they mixed paints with oil and used them as lotions.

When Indians met Europeans they were heavily painted. They wore black, white, red, yellow, and blue paints.

16

Indians got pigments for their paints from the material around them. The colors red and yellow came from the mineral called ocher found in the earth. Black was made from the mineral graphite or from charcoal soot. These materials were ground into a powder in a paint cup, mixed with oils, and used to decorate themselves and to decorate canoes and weapons.

Colors also came from plants. For example, they boiled the leaves and bark of a cedar for olive green, white maple for light blue, ash bark for yellow, pine or hemlock for brown. They got other colors from berries and roots.

How did they dress?

Indians dressed lightly and simply in summer and winter. The every day, work-a-day piece of clothing was the deerskin loincloth. For women it was more like a small apron.

In cold weather they put other deerskin clothes over the loincloth.

They wore robes, long leggings, and moccasins. When the weather was freezing, they wore fur-lined robes with the fur next to their skin. Or, they draped fur skins like blankets over their clothes.

They had no pockets in their clothes. They hung small pouches of snakeskin or deerskin from their waists or over their shoulders. In these they carried their paints, fats, food, or tools.

Occasionally a robe or shirt was made of woven hemp and grass.

What did they wear on special occasions?

People dressed up in decorated clothes and bright ornaments for special occasions.

A woman put on her long wraparound skirt and jacket and her beaded moccasins. She twined bright red and yellow plant fibers into her hair and she stuck a bright bird feather into her snakeskin headband.

Around her neck she wore large pendants made of stone, bone, or shell. Or she put on a string of beads made of animal teeth. From her ears she dangled pendant earrings. She put on her make-up—red paints on her cheeks, temples, and forehead and black pigment for eyeshadow around her eyes.

A man dressed up in his mantle made of deerskin, moose, or bearskin. Sometimes it was made of iridescent wild turkey feathers. He slung the mantle under the right arm and clasped it over the left shoulder. In freezing weather he put a fur skin over the bare right arm.

Men, too, wore large pendants and beads around their necks and put on ornamental armbands and anklebands. They stuck one, two, or three feathers into their hair and hung pendants from a beaded headband.

How did they make their ornaments?

They often used the bright feathers of wild birds for decoration. They got red feathers from a woodpecker, green from a mallard, orange from an oriole, brown from a thrush, and white from a heron. Or they dyed porcupine quills red or yellow or blue and sewed them on their garments. They also made embroidery of birds, flowers, and animals with colored plant fibers.

Perhaps the most popular fashion was to cut fringe on skirts, jackets, moccasins, and leggings.

When they wanted to use beads, they had to make them. These beads were called wampum or in Algonquian, *wompompeage.*

Wampum was made all year, but often women and children gathered clam- and whelk shells during the summer and stored them. In stormy winter weather when men were indoors they made tiny flat beads from the insides of these shells.

Purple beads were made from small chips of clamshells. White beads were made from the inner tube or stem of the whelk shell. They carefully drilled a hole on each side of these shell pieces with a sharp pointed tool until the two holes met. Then they smoothed these little beads down on a special stone.

Wampum was valuable. It had many uses. Important events were recorded in belts of wampum by arranging the beads in a special design. White belts of wampum were given as presents and peace offerings. Dark belts were sent to challenge enemies or declare war. Strings of beads were used to send messages and to identify the messenger. And wampum was used as money in trade.

How were animal skins made into clothing?

When hunters killed animals, they removed the skins with sharp stone blades or arrowheads. They rolled up these skins and took them home.

Women scraped all the fat, hair, and flesh off the tough animal skins. As they scraped these hides they softened them.

They soaked the hides in oil for a few days and then washed them. Oil helped make them weatherproof.

In a room heated by a good fire, women wrung out the skins and pulled and stretched them until soft and dry. Sometimes skins were put on a stretching frame and rubbed with a rounded stick until they were soft.

Finally the skins were smoked or "tanned" over a fire called a smudge fire.

The skins were sewn up "like a bag." The open side was placed over a funnel under which there was a fire of oak, cedar, or birch bark. Smoking helped preserve the skins, and the smoke from different woods varied the colors from light to dark brown.

Women cut these "tanned" soft skins into moccasins, skirts, leggings, shirts, and other clothing. With a bone needle and thin strips of leather, they sewed them together and added ornaments.

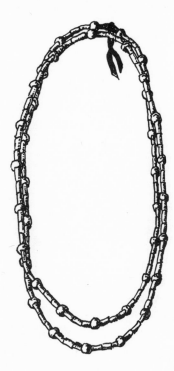

ORNAMENTS

24

What Did They Eat?

THE INDIANS ATE THE MEAT OF ANIMALS most of the year. Usually it was deer meat. But they also ate bear, beaver, moose and even bison meat.

When possible they added wild turkey, ducks and geese.

Flocks of pigeons and crows were shot down when food was scarce.

In spring, summer, and fall there was an abundance of other food. There were the vegetables they planted —corn, beans, squash and pumpkin. And there were the wild fruits and berries growing all around them.

Men and older boys brought in fish. People living near the bay had lobsters, clams, and oysters.

And when the first frost loosened nuts from trees, children helped their mothers gather them.

They also dug up roots and ate eels and snakes.

How did they cook their food?

Women roasted, boiled, and dried their food over the open fire. They also baked food in clay pots or in leaves over hot coals.

They kept a stew of mixed foods cooking all the time.

Sometimes it was a stew of fresh meat and vegetables flavored with nuts and berries.

At other times it was a mixture of dried acorns, some strips of dried meat and fish. Or just a root.

People who lived near the bay made a seafood chowder or they broiled clams and oysters over a fire.

When corn was in season, they cooked all kinds of corn dishes. Some of them we eat today.

They mixed corn with beans into succotash. They made hominy, popcorn, and roast corn-on-the-cob. They ground corn into cornmeal and "baked" corn bread and corn cakes sweetened with maple sugar or fresh strawberries.

They mashed parched kernels of corn into meal, called *Nokake* or *Yokeg*. It was a journey cake, rich and nourishing when eaten with water.

Indian warriors and hunters carried *Nokake* in their pouches when they had to be on the trail. It was often their only food for three, four, or five days at a time.

Did the family eat together?

There were no rules about when a person had to eat. You ate when you were hungry.

You helped yourself to food from the stewpot with the large wooden ladle nearby. You put the food into your own wood bowl, sat down near the fire, and ate.

There were no forks and spoons. You ate with your fingers.

Indians shared their food with neighbors and strangers. When people entered a village they were immediately offered a bowl of food. It was rude to refuse to eat.

Men and women would get up during the night and prepare a sleeping mat and food for anyone who came to their wigwam. It was a rule of hospitality observed by all tribes.

How did they preserve food?

When there was plenty of corn, fish, meat, and nuts, women preserved whatever food they could against winter shortages.

When corn became ripe, women set ears of corn out to dry each day in the sun. They carefully protected the corn from dampness and rain. When the corn was dried, they placed it in tightly woven baskets. Around

QUAIL

TURKEY

27

the baskets they wrapped strong mats and stored them in the ground. These storage holes in the ground were their barns.

When the Indians had extra squash and pumpkins, they cut them into strips and hung them on racks to dry.

In the hunting season, meat was cut into strips and dried in smoke. Smoked moose tongue was often eaten.

Fish were hung on a rack to dry over a slow fire. Or they placed fish and shellfish on a plank of wood to dry in the sun.

Berries and nuts were dried the same way.

When snow and ice covered the earth and they had no fresh food, the Indians dug up their corn, and they ate dried pieces of meat, fish, and vegetables stored in baskets.

Why Was Hunting Important?

THE INDIAN HAD TO HUNT TO EAT. When hunting was poor, people were hungry.

After the last corn was picked in the fall until fish filled the streams in the spring, meat was the basic food.

Men were the hunters. They were busy all year either hunting or preparing for it, sharpening stone blades, shaping arrowheads, working over a new bow, building a canoe.

The land gave them their food and they knew every part of the land. They knew every mountain and stream and winding trail. They knew the habits of animals, where they gathered, what they ate, and when they slept.

According to their religion the land was filled with invisible spirits that lived in everything in nature. These

spirits protected them and made them feel at home in the woodlands. Before the hunt the Indians appealed to these spirits for help. After the hunt, they thanked these spirits in special dances and ceremonies.

Indians killed only what they needed in order to live. And they used every part of an animal. Nothing was wasted. They used skins for clothing, furs for warmth, antlers and bones for tools, tendons for cord, gut and intestine for pouches and bags.

How did they hunt?

They stalked animals. They trapped and snared

30

them. They built enclosures and shot them with bow and arrow or killed them with short, sharp daggers or long spears.

Sometimes a man hunted alone. Usually the Indians hunted in groups of twelve, twenty, or thirty men.

What happened when a man went out to kill a deer?

It often took a man two or three days to bring in a deer.

First he had to find one.

He looked for the deer's hoofprints. Or he tried to catch one crossing a trail. He tried to surprise one while it was feeding or while it was sleeping in the very early dawn. Sometimes he imitated the bleating sounds of a lost fawn. He hoped the parents would come out into the open.

When he finally saw a deer, he followed it through the woods until he got close enough to shoot it with his bow and arrow.

At last he returned to his family. Slung across his shoulders in a burden strap was the dead deer.

What other ways did they hunt animals?

In spring and summer men watched where deer were gathering. In the fall, after the harvest, 200 to 300 men organized drives against the deer.

They sped in canoes up rivers or by foot along trails to the hunting ground.

They enclosed two to three miles of land with fences into the shape of a funnel or a V. One group of men drove the animals into the broad opening of the funnel toward the narrow section. There other Indians shot them with arrows.

At night the men set snares in the enclosure to trap animals. A noose was attached to a pegged down sapling. Acorns were used as bait. As soon as the animal ate the acorns, the noose tightened and the sapling sprang up catching the deer in the noose. The deer hung in the air, the noose tightened around his neck or leg or antlers. In the dawn the Indians cut the deer down and killed it.

Snares also trapped wolves, foxes, and wild cats. Their skins were used for warmth. They were not eaten.

Indians did not eat animals that fed on other animals. They only ate animals that fed on plants.

Did women and children help?

Women and children helped by checking deer traps each day.

In the fall, some families went with the men to the hunting grounds. They traveled fifty or sixty miles from their villages and stayed away two or three months. They lived in bark hunting houses where they stored and dried the meat. Often the women helped skin, clean, and pack the meat right where the animals were killed.

Each day women and children checked as many as forty traps set in deer paths and near freshwater springs. They had to reach trapped animals before wolves and other animals ate them. Sometimes women and children found a half-eaten deer or just some bones strewn about.

Hunting families tried to get back to their villages before the heavy snows fell. There were no wagons, carts, or animals to carry them and their burdens. Men, women, and older children shouldered the heavy packs of meat. They wore snowshoes to get through the harsh snowed-in woods. Some had sleds or drags which were harnessed to backs and shoulders and pulled.

When families finally returned, there was great rejoicing. People feasted on the fresh supply of meat.

Why did they use bows and arrows?
Didn't they have guns?

Indians had not yet discovered the use of metal. They had no iron.

34

They made their tools and implements out of stone, wood, shoulder blades, antlers, animal bones, and shells. These they patiently chipped, scraped, and shaped into a needed tool. With these tools they were able to make delicate baskets as well as sturdy canoes.

How did they make bows and arrows?

They shaped a bow from a slender single piece of wood. They used branches from many different trees, such as hickory, witch hazel, oak, beech, or rock maple. They heated the wood over a slow fire. They oiled it, polished it, and heated it again. Gradually they bent it into shape.

At each end of the bow they cut notches for the bowstrings. These were made of three or four twists of animal skin or the tendons of an animal. Men decorated their bows with paints and carvings. When finished a bow stood three or four feet high.

Arrows had to be straight. They were made from dry, seasoned wood; otherwise they wobbled when shot from the bow.

They cut down and shaped arrows from slender branches of hickory, ash, or white oak. They also used reeds and elder tree branches. To one end of the arrowshaft they tied the feathers that kept the arrow straight on its course. Some used eagle or vulture feathers. Others used crow or hawk feathers. At the other end of the arrowshaft they inserted a stone flint

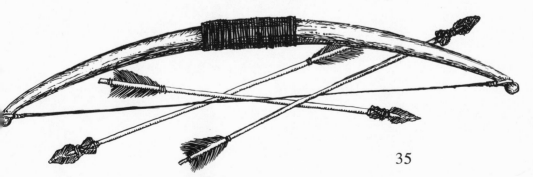

35

arrowhead and tied it down with a strip of leather. The arrowhead, usually triangular in shape, had a sharp point that could penetrate the skin of an animal. Often after killing an animal, hunters removed the arrowshaft, leaving the arrowhead in the animal's body. They took the arrowshafts home with them where they fitted them with new arrowheads to be used again for hunting.

CHIPPING

FLAKING

FINISHING

MAKING AN ARROWHEAD

How Did They Farm?

WOMEN WERE THE FARMERS.

They broke up the soil, planted the seeds, pulled the weeds, and picked the crops.

"When the leaves of the white oak are as big as the ears of a mouse," it was time to plant corn.

Then women set to work. They used a stick or a bone to break up the soil. Or they attached a shell to a stick and used it as a hoe. Sometimes they used the shoulder blades of a bear, moose, or deer tied to wooden handles. When there was nothing else around, they used their hands.

Every three feet, women made small mounds of earth. Into each mound they put fish as fertilizer. Then they dropped in some kernels of corn. Into the same mound they planted seeds of beans, squash, and pumpkins.

Women worked hard in their gardens. When crops were good tribes could settle in one place for five months, from April to September. Then they had to move to be near game.

Children helped their mothers. They pulled out weeds. And they helped shoo away thousands of birds that swooped down and ate the crops.

Tobacco was planted and taken care of by men.

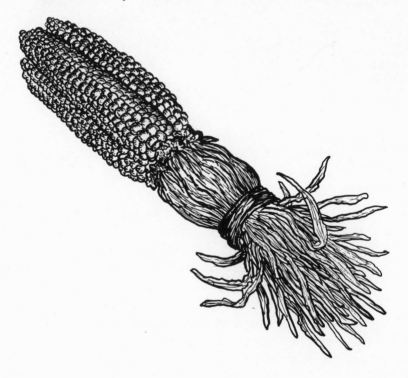

How Did They Fish?

THERE WAS PLENTY OF FISH in spring, summer, and fall.

There was so much codfish in the bay that it gave Cape Cod its name.

Indians used nets, spears, bows and arrows, hooks, lines with sinkers, or their bare hands to catch fish.

From canoes on rivers and bays, they harpooned fish with sharp spears. Or they cast nets to catch freshwater bass, salmon, sturgeon, or mackerel. They swooped up saltwater mackerel and haddock in nets.

"When lightning bugs begin to appear late in June," it is time to spear salmon. They fished for salmon at night. Torches were used to lure the fish to the surface of the water. Then they speared them or shot them with bow and arrow.

Often they built enclosures at the bottom of the falls of a river and on the bay to trap fish.

Even in cold wet weather, Indians spent the night near the water to search their nets for fish. After a winter of meat and some dried nuts and corn, fish baked in hot coals was a delicious treat.

Occasionally they brought in a whale that they harpooned from a large dugout canoe. This huge seagoing mammal was cut up and sent around to the neighbors as gifts.

What Was a Village Like?

A VILLAGE WAS A CLUSTER OF WIGWAMS built close to each other near fresh water and food. Sometimes you would see a busy village. A month later the village would disappear.

Villages were put up and taken down with the change in season. Or, if there was a disaster like sickness or drought, the village was taken apart.

Whenever a band of people decided to change its dwelling place, they moved on together. Then they set up another village.

A village was more than its wigwams. It was the band of people who lived in it. About one hundred people lived and worked together in a village like one very large family.

Wherever the people lived, a village took shape. It was the center of work and pleasure. Everyone shared

41

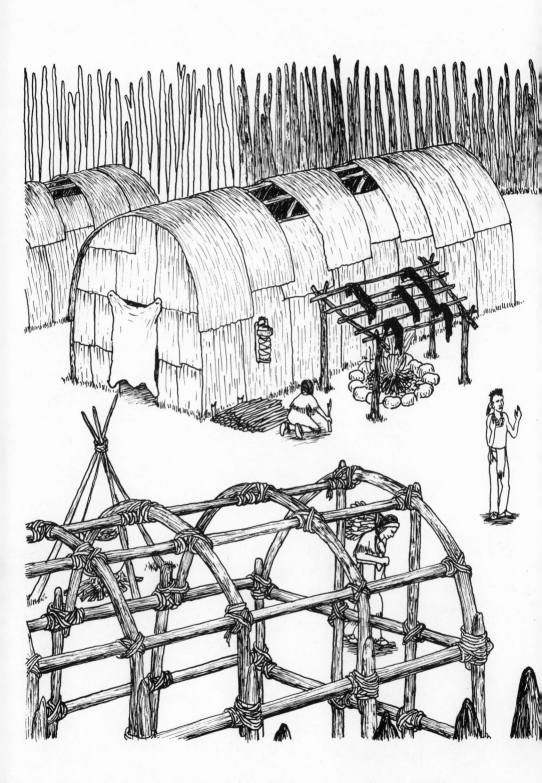

everything—good and bad. When there was food, everyone ate. When there was no food, everyone went hungry. In sickness they took care of each other. In good times they enjoyed themselves.

They were a friendly and generous people. Anyone passing through a village was always offered food and a place to sleep.

People worked alongside each other. Men built canoes, shaped tools, prepared weapons for war or hunting. Women prepared food, made clothes, mats and baskets, or did the farming.

A whole village turned out to clear a new field for planting. Young and old, men and women, each had his job. While men chopped down thick trees with stone axes, women and children gathered branches and vines for burning. Grandparents watched the babies.

Backbreaking work seemed lighter because it was festive. People joked and sang as they worked.

Sometimes village people just sat around to gossip and exchange the news. Often they relaxed by playing games. Men and women enjoyed races. Men played football, lacrosse, hockey, and handball. They also liked to gamble. They shot dice with painted pebbles or nuts and they played cards with cards made of rush.

Many times during the year people gathered together for special religious ceremonies at which they thanked their Creator for his help and protection. These events often marked the change in season or the planting, ripening, and gathering of food. In the early spring there was the Maple festival when the maple tree was tapped for its syrup, and the Planting festival when corn seeds were planted in garden plots. In summer there was the Green Corn ceremony when the first ears of corn were eaten. There were hunters' songs and dances in the fall and a great Thanksgiving feast at the

LACROSSE
STICK

44

gathering of the harvest. There were mid-winter ceremonies when the countryside was covered with snow.
People sang and danced at these festivals in the ancient
ways handed down through the ages.

What kind of houses did they have?

A wigwam or *wikwam* is the Algonquian word for
house. It was shaped like a dome.

The man built the frame of the house out of tall, thin
tree trunks called saplings. He firmly set about eight or
ten saplings into the ground about two feet apart to
form a half-circle. He set the same number on the other
side. He then arched the matching pairs together and
tied them with strong narrow strips of bark, root fibers,
or hemp twine.

To make the framework stronger, the man lashed
more saplings across the arched saplings.

The woman took over the rest of the work. She covered the framework with overlapping pieces of bark or
strong mats. Light birch bark was used in the summer.
Heavy elm or walnut bark was used in the winter. Mats
made of rush or cornhusks were sewn together with
bone needles and hemp thread. The splinter bones of a
crane made fine needles.

The small door of the wigwam was also a mat or a
piece of bark. An opening was left at the top for smoke
to escape from the indoor fire.

These bark-covered houses looked like thatched huts
huddled close to each other. They were often cold,
smoky, and crowded in winter and hot and stuffy in
summer.

Strong tribes had palisaded villages for protection
against enemy attack. These villages were enclosed by a
series of closely set tree trunks about twelve feet high.

How did the inside of the house look?

The wigwam had one room. In it the family slept, cooked, ate, and worked.

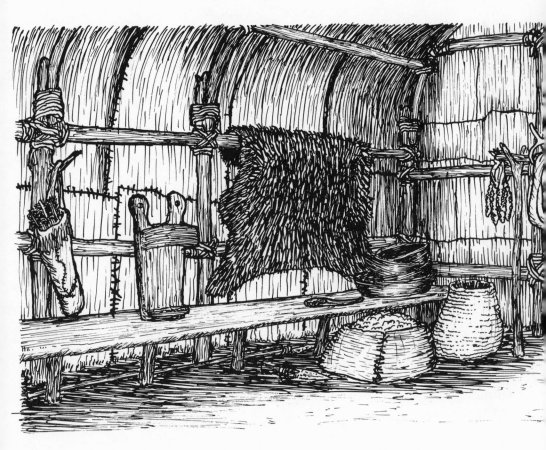

Colorful mats decorated the inside walls. Hanging from the walls were baskets of all sizes and shapes made from any material at hand. There were baskets of bark, hemp, rush, woodsplints, cornhusks, tall grasses, or plant fibers. They were used like pantry shelves for storage. Women stored seeds, corn, dried meat, fish, paints, or other household items in them.

Also hanging on the walls were deers' feet, or stags' horns, or eagles' claws. These were symbols of their religion.

Along the sides of the walls about twelve inches off the ground were benches. They were made of small tree trunks lashed together and covered with mats or fur skins. People sat on them during the day and slept on them at night. Extra people slept on mats around the fire.

The fire was set in a small hollow surrounded by stones in the center of the room. It gave warmth and light and provided a fire for cooking.

Near the fire were pots and pans made of bark, wood, clay, or stone. There were large and small wood bowls. There were wood paddles, ladles, and mortars and pestles carved out of strong burls of wood. A birch bark pail stood nearby filled with water.

Sometimes two, three, or four families shared one large wigwam. Each family had an open fire in the center of its area. Women talked with each other as they took care of the house.

Why did they move around so much?

Indians set up homes to be near food and fresh water.

In the spring they moved near rivers and lakes and the ocean shore to get the first run of fish to fill the waters.

In the summer they set up homes to be close to planting fields.

In the fall they moved to sheltered valleys. Or they moved to bark-covered hunting shelters to be near game.

They also changed wigwams often.

When someone in the family died and they felt too much grief, they moved out of their house and set up another one.

When a house became too full of insects and fleas, they moved their belongings to other quarters. And when the tribe was at war, and the enemy near the village, they deserted their homes and hid in the tall grasses of nearby swamps.

When they moved, they left the framework of the wigwam standing and took the mats and other household belongings with them.

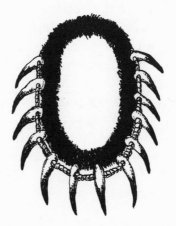

What Were Children Like?

CHILDREN RAN FREELY AROUND THE VILLAGE. They were loved and watched over not only by their parents but by all grown-ups. So long as there was food and shelter any place in the tribe, children were taken care of.

There were no baby-sitters. Children went wherever mama and papa went.

A new baby was strapped onto a cradleboard and kept close to the mother. When she worked in the garden, she hung the cradleboard on the branch of a nearby tree. When she went from one place to another, she strapped the cradleboard onto her back. This way the baby could see what was going on.

As children were growing, they explored their surroundings. Sometimes they got hurt, but no one coddled them. They cried and got over it. And they learned from the experience.

Boys ran around with no clothes until ten or twelve years of age. Girls wore little loincloths like small aprons. They had short hair. When they started to wear clothes, they dressed like their parents, and let their hair grow long.

Did they go to school?

There were no schools. Indians had not yet developed an alphabet and they had no written language. There were no books and no reading and writing.

Yet children learned many, many things. How did they learn? They learned by listening to their parents and other grown-ups. They learned by watching and copying the way things were done. And they learned by doing things themselves.

What did children learn?

Children learned the history, arts, and customs of their people. And they learned how to take care of themselves and how to be at home in the woodlands.

They found out which plants they could eat and which would make them sick. They knew a rattlesnake might kill them and a garter snake could become a pet. They felt how sharp a claw or bone tool could be and how hot a fire was.

They could run almost as soon as they could walk and at the age of two their fathers taught them how to swim and later how to paddle and steer a canoe.

Children did their share of work. Older ones helped bring in food. They used sticks to kill small animals like squirrels, rabbits, and raccoons. They helped pull in nets laden with fish.

Boys helped their fathers. They learned to strip the bark off the white birch tree and to sew it over the

50

frame of a canoe. They helped make arrowheads and axes and knives by learning how to chip and shape stone flint.

Girls were their mothers' helpers. They cut meat into strips for drying and learned to make twine out of plant fibers. They learned to plant crops and how to prepare food.

Children listened to village elders tell stories about their ancestors. At religious ceremonials they watched young men perform special dances.

They observed and were part of all the activity around them. In this way they picked up their skills and got to know their history without going to a special school.

What games did they play?

They ran races. They ran and ran and ran. Their legs became strong and their bodies became strong and limber.

They ran around the village playing leapfrog and follow-the-leader. Their one pet, a dog, ran along with them.

A thick stick was used as a bat to hit balls made of stone, wood, or animal skin. Sometimes just a pine cone or a large seed served as a ball.

They played darts with real feathers from a goose or a swan. They played spin-the-top. The top was shaped from wood, stone, or bone. It was a favorite game. They watched it spin dizzily on a frozen pond in winter.

In summer they tried their luck at fishing in a nearby pond with a fishhook shaped from a bone. In winter they hiked on snowshoes and went sliding on icy slopes.

There were wooden dolls to dress in deerskin clothes, and feathers, stones, nuts, seeds, and bones to use as toys. Practice with bow and arrow was started at an early age.

Whatever children did, they tried to do well. As they grew up they began to understand that their lives depended on the skills, endurance, and courage they were learning through games.

What Was a Tribe?

A TRIBE WAS AN INDEPENDENT NATION. It had its own land, its own leaders, and its own language.

It was made up of the bands of people in the many small villages scattered on tribal land. The people shared the land in common. They were free to move about, to hunt, fish, or set up new homes.

The largest, strongest tribes were in southern New England. Some tribes, such as the Narragansett, had as many as 4,000 people. Other strong tribes were the Wampanoags, the Pequots, and the Mohegans. The people of these tribes were farmers as well as hunters. This made it possible for them to stay in one place for part of the year.

The tribes of the north, such as the Abnaki and the Penacooks, were hunters, wandering over the land all year in search of game.

Who was the head of the tribe?

He was the sachem. People did not vote for him. There were no elections.

The sachem inherited his role. It was handed down from father to son. If there were no sons, then other members of the family could become leaders.

The sachem was spokesman for his tribe. He was usually an able and wise man who looked after the welfare of his people. He was brave in war and one of the best marksmen in the hunt.

A council of village leaders helped him make important decisions. They decided serious matters such as war and peace, alliances with other tribes, and when to call in the religious leader.

There was hardly ever robbery or murder among the Woodland people but when there was, the sachem handed down the punishment, usually death or exile.

He entertained all visitors with great hospitality. Strangers and friends were brought to his home, usually in a palisaded village, where he was a generous host and provided food and places to sleep. This was tradition in all tribes.

On special occasions he dressed in great splendor with beaded cap and beaded mantle. A heavy wampum belt girdled his waist. He wore ceremonial paints on his face as did his councilors.

People of the tribe supported the sachem. They sent him a share of their hunt, their fish, and their crops. Or, if he dominated weak tribes, he collected tribute from them in the form of food, furs, and wampum.

The sachems of the four important New England tribes in early Colonial times were:

TOMAHAWK

Sachem	Tribe	Area
Massasoit and his son Metacomet known as King Philip	Wampanoag	Mass.
Canonicus, his nephew Miantanimo, and his son Canonchet	Narragansett	R.I.
Sassacus	Pequot	Conn.
Uncas	Mohegan	Conn.

56

It was Chief Massasoit and the Wampanoag tribe who helped the Pilgrims when they landed in Plymouth.

Were there Indian wars?

There were many wars between tribes.

Tribes went to war when their hunting grounds were invaded or to settle boundary disputes. Sometimes an insult to a leader started a war.

Indians fought with bow and arrow, wooden war club, and tomahawk. Some tribes used spears.

Battles were not very bloody. They did not fight to destroy each other. Rarely did they attack each other's villages. When they fought in the woods, they used trees as shields. When they fought in the open, they leaped and danced about to avoid being hit. A warrior would shoot his arrow at an enemy and then watch where it fell before he shot another.

A battle often stopped when a warrior was wounded or killed. His tribesmen wanted to take him home. The enemy wanted him as a prize.

Victorious tribes took captives. Some men died a terrible death by torture. This was considered an honorable way to die, to endure physical pain. Others, especially women and children, were put to work as household servants. Eventually they were adopted into the tribe.

WAR CLUB

There was no scalping in the early days of intertribal warfare. No one knows for sure whether the Indian or the white man introduced scalping. It was not known to be an Indian custom before the whites arrived and began to pay for Indian scalps.

What kind of religion did they have?

Indians believed in one Creator. He showed himself through the Spirit of Nature, through animals, birds, earth, children, sun, fire, and hunting.

Indians had deep faith in the Creator and in their Mother Earth.

When they needed sun to ripen their crops they appealed to the spirit of the sun. When children were ill, they appealed to the spirit that heals children and gives children strength.

In times of great calamity like drought, flood, disease, the religious leader, the medicine man, was called

in. He was trained from childhood for his role. Sometimes he fasted and had visions. Through him the Creator showed his power.

For a special religious dance, the medicine man dressed in the skins of an animal. He painted his face with special colors and sang and danced according to ancient custom.

While he danced, people sang out their sorrows. Some sacrificed everything they had. They threw weapons, fur hides, food, and ornaments onto the fire.

In this way they hoped to be forgiven for the evil acts they thought had brought on the terrible punishment.

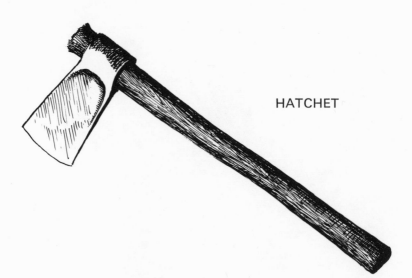

HATCHET

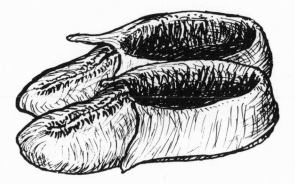

What Was the Language Like?

EVERY TIME YOU SAY MOCCASIN you are using an Indian word. When you say wigwam, squash, tobacco, raccoon, poncho, you are using Indian words.

Many Indian words have been adopted into our language. We have used some in this book. Hickory, moose, raccoon, succotash, hominy. There are thousands of other words.

Almost half the states, cities, rivers, and mountains in New England have Indian names. These place-names have meanings. They describe a place so other people can find it.

Connecticut means land "on the long tidal river."

Massachusetts—"at the place of great hills."

Housatonic—"stream over the mountain."

Narragansett—"at the small narrow point."

Nantucket—"in the midst of waters."

Pawtucket—"at the falls in the river."

Penobscot—"at the falling rocks."

Were the languages difficult?

They were very difficult languages. They had large vocabularies and definite grammars.

Since there was no written language, the spoken language did all the work. The Indians passed on to children their long history, folk stories, and traditions—all in the spoken word. Words were bold, colorful, and rich in meaning. They were often poetic. Indians were known as good orators.

Did all the tribes speak the same language?

No, they didn't. If you traveled from one tribe to another you would hear different languages. Yet many were enough alike so that people of different tribes in New England understood each other. The languages were like different branches of one big tree. They were

all part of the Algonquian family of languages. To speak to Indians from other parts of the country, hand "sign" language was used.

Here are some Indian words. They are in Narragan-sett.

friend	Nétop
peace	Aquène
sit down	Máttapsh
I cannot	Non ânum

Or you can count:

one	Nquít
two	Neèsse
three	Nìsh
four	Yôh
five	Napànna

Then you can say:

farewell!	Hawúnshech

How Did They Travel?

THE INDIANS TRAVELED ON FOOT AND BY CANOE.

A man could run 100 miles in a single day. He could run 50 miles to deliver an urgent message and back to his village the same day.

They used the narrow winding trails that wound through the woodlands. These paths were always kept free from underbrush. They formed a belt of travel and communication between villages and tribes.

Families trudged along these paths single file when they moved from summer to winter villages. The man walked first. In his left hand he carried his bow and over his left shoulder was his quiver of arrows. His right hand was free, ready to protect his family from attack by animals and enemies.

Women and children followed, laden down with baskets and hemp bags. In these were the family belongings.

What kind of canoes did they have?

Canoes were light. They moved rapidly and quietly on rivers and sea.

The birch bark canoe was so light, people carried it over land from one river to the next. On a rough sea it looked like a "wind-driven" ship as it scudded from wave to wave.

It was made of tender young pine saplings set close together like ribs. The ends were pulled together and tied with tough fibers or roots of trees. They sewed sheets of birch bark to each other and to the frame. To make it watertight, they applied pitch from pine trees to the seams.

The dugout canoe could carry thirty to forty people. It was used in sea battles or to move families. Often it carried men to hunting sites.

The dugout was made from one single huge tree trunk. They cut down their tallest, broadest pine or chestnut tree. After removing bark and branches, they

charred one whole side of this huge log with fire or red hot stones. Using seashells and bone scrapers, they scraped and charred the log, over and over, until they finally hollowed it into shape.

We still use canoes like theirs. And there are still some original Indian trails in wooded mountains of New England.

DAGGER

What Happened to the Woodland Indians?

WOODLAND INDIANS HAVE ALMOST ALL DISAPPEARED. Their strength and independence were broken by sickness and wars.

Indians living along the Atlantic coast were the first to meet white explorers and settlers. They were the first

to catch their infectious diseases. They caught small-pox, measles, and typhoid. They had no resistance to these diseases and there were no medicines with which to treat them.

Sometimes these epidemics raged through their villages. Thousands and thousands died. Whole tribes were wiped out.

Woodland Indians were also the first to be killed in wars between Indians and whites. In two fierce wars the powerful tribes of Massachusetts, Connecticut, and Rhode Island were destroyed.

In 1637 there was the Pequot War. The Pequot Indians of Connecticut, under Chief Sassacus, fought alone against the English settlers who were slowly moving into their land. But they were no match for the English. The English used muskets and swords. Many were protected by head and chest armor. They were well organized and their military leaders were trained in the brutal wars of Europe.

The Indians hardly had a chance to use their bows and arrows. In one horrible act 600 Indian men, women, and children were killed when the English set fire to their palisaded village in Mystic. Flames quickly spread to all 70 wigwams. The whole palisaded village was turned into a blazing oven. Those who tried to escape were slain by the sword.

Indians did not know war could kill so many. They learned how powerful the English were.

After the Pequot War, in which most of the tribe was wiped out, English settlers quickly took over their land in Connecticut.

The English were increasing their rule over the lands and lives of the Indians. Colonies were springing up all over New England, pushing the Indians out. To the English the Indians were "savages," inferior to the whites. The English became the masters, treating the Indians as their subjects. They "bought up" land. They "summoned" Indian leaders to meetings. Indians were tried in English courts. Missionaries were teaching them to become Christians.

Indians saw their freedom and culture rapidly eaten away. The white man was trying to change them and rule them instead of accepting them as equal and independent.

After many bloody and brutal incidents, the Indians decided to defend themselves. This led to King Philip's

War in 1675. King Philip was not really a king but the English name given to Metacomet, son of Massasoit. This time Indians got together. Metacomet, leader of the Wampanoags, was helped by Canonchet, leader of the Narragansetts, and by other tribes. The Indians now had some guns and ammunition.

The war started with a raid on the colonial village of Swansea, Massachusetts, in June, 1675. It was the beginning of a terrible cruel struggle that lasted over a year.

Indians raided villages and ambushed colonists in fields and on roads. They completely destroyed many towns. Hundreds of English men, women, and children were killed. They were killed with guns and tomahawks or trapped in burning homes. A few became captives of the Indians.

Again the Indians were no match for the English. They were finally defeated.

In both wars Indians were hunted and rounded up. Old men, women, and children were cut down as they hid in swamps. They were captured and killed as they tried to flee to other tribes. Hundreds of captives, including the wife and nine-year-old son of Metacomet, were sold to the slave markets in the West Indies. Some women and young girls were made servants in New England homes. Some escaped to tribes in the west.

When Canonchet was captured and about to be put to death, he said, "I like it well. I shall die before my heart is soft, before I have spoken anything unworthy of myself."

Metacomet was tracked down and finally captured in a swamp near his village on Mount Hope. He was put to death in August, 1676. This brought the war to an end. And it brought Indian tribal life in New England to an end, too.

INDIANS TAKEN CAPTIVE FOR SLAVE MARKET

In both wars the Mohegan Indians, under Chief Uncas, helped the English. But in time their lands were bought up and their lives changed.

Indian wars continued in Maine for many years. Finally the Abnaki, Penobscot, and Etchimin tribes were defeated. Many fled to Canada.

Some Indians who escaped slowly drifted back to their tribal grounds. But the land which was part of their lives now belonged to the English. The life they knew no longer existed. There were no Indian villages dotting lakes and streams. English settlers, shaping a new life, excluded Indians from taking part in it. Indians had no rights, could not vote, and were denied education and jobs. They became a homeless, poor, and neglected people. For hundreds of years they have been outcasts in their own land.

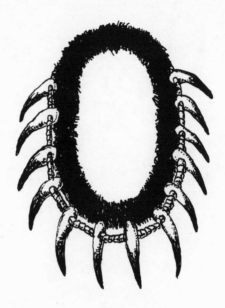

Are There Indians in New England Today?

IT IS HARD TO KNOW HOW MANY INDIANS are living in New England today. Some say there are 6,000. Others say there are 10,000 or more. Among them are Woodland Indians, descendants of the tribes that once lived in the dense forests. Many come from other tribes. Among them are Micmac, Malecite, Mohawk, Sioux, and Cherokee. Few are full-blooded Indians.

Indians have adjusted in different ways to the modern world. Some have "assimilated." They live like white Americans. Many cluster together in their own communities in small villages. Others live on reservations. An increasing number of Indians are moving to large cities where they hope to find jobs. There are Indian writers, painters, teachers, musicians, scientists,

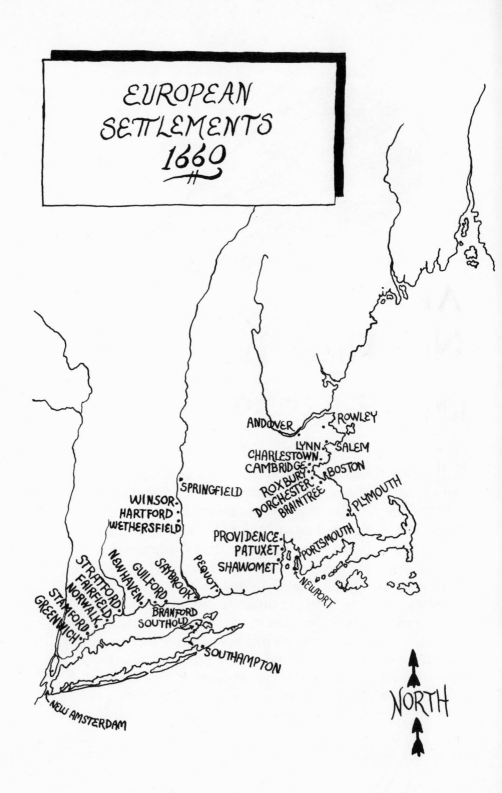

EUROPEAN
SETTLEMENTS
1660

ANDOVER · · ROWLEY
LYNN · · SALEM
CHARLESTOWN ·
CAMBRIDGE ·
· SPRINGFIELD   ROXBURY · · BOSTON
                       DORCHESTER ·
WINSOR ·   BRAINTREE · · PLYMOUTH
HARTFORD ·
WETHERSFIELD ·   PROVIDENCE ·
                       PATUXET ·   PORTSMOUTH
            SAYBROOK   SHAWOMET ·
STRATFORD · NEW HAVEN · PEQUOT ·
FAIRFIELD · GUILFORD ·   NEWPORT
NORWALK ·
STAMFORD · · BRANFORD
GREENWICH · SOUTHOLD

· SOUTHAMPTON

· NEW AMSTERDAM

NORTH

workers, and businessmen. A few are successful. They own their own homes and have cars. The largest number of Indians have no jobs at all or they have poor jobs. No matter where they are and what they do, Indians are proud of their Indian heritage.

Most Indians, especially those in large cities like Boston, find life very difficult. They are discriminated against because they are Indian and because their skin is brown. They are still considered "inferior" in the white man's world. Few jobs are open to them. They have poor housing and no money. And their health and education have been neglected.

Indians find life a little easier on reservations. They have a sense of freedom on land that is theirs. They can live a little as their ancestors did. They take care of each other and still share everything even though there is not much to share.

What are reservations?

Reservations are sections of land set aside— "reserved"—for use by an Indian tribe. These are small parts of their original homelands.

In New England each state supervises its own reservations. In other parts of the United States reservations are run by the federal government.

Most people on reservations do not pay rent or taxes on their land. Usually the state government has a few funds set aside to help maintain reservation land and housing.

Reservations vary in size. There is a tiny one, perhaps the smallest in the country, in Trumbull, Connecticut. It is only about the size of half a city block. On it an Indian man and his wife live.

In Kent, Connecticut, there is the large, parklike

Schagticoke Reservation on which only a few people now live.

There are two large reservations for the Pequot Indians in Connecticut. One reservation is in Ledyard

Town and another is in North Stonington. A handful of elderly people live on them. These reservations are not marked off. The land is scrubby and rocky. You cannot tell whether the small frame houses and trailers are the homes of Indians. You can see men fishing from boats on nearby lakes. Perhaps they are Pequots who, like their ancestors, are hoping for a catch of fish for the day's food.

Massachusetts has one reservation on which one family lives.

The largest reservations in New England are in Maine. The Penobscot tribe owns about 140 islands in the Penobscot river. Over 600 Penobscot Indians occupy only one of these islands. It is called Indian Island at Old Town.

About 500 Passamaquoddy Indians live on two reservations in Maine. One is called Pleasant Point Reservation and is in Perry. The other is the Indian Township Reservation in Princeton.

Most children attend the one elementary school on each reservation. Those who graduate can go to high schools off the reservation. But reservation schools do not teach them their own history and do not prepare them for high school in the white world.

As a result, Indian children find life and school in the white world confusing. No one bothers to understand their special background. They are looked down upon and made to feel inferior.

Children drop out of school at a very early age. Few get high school diplomas. Very few go on to college.

Men work in nearby mills and shipyards. Many get seasonal work as loggers for lumber companies. But jobs for Indians are scarce. That is why so many young people leave the reservations for large cities. They dream that life in the cities will be better.

The Tribal Councils on each Maine reservation, now elected by the people, are trying to get improved living conditions. They are trying to get small industries started to provide jobs for their people and to make themselves independent.

They also want the history and languages of their people taught in reservation and other schools.

THANKSGIVING DAY, 1970

Who Are the "New Indians?"

INDIANS TODAY ARE SPEAKING OUT. They are telling Americans their problems. They are telling their side of history. There are new voices in New England as there are throughout the country.

Tribes are no longer enemies. Algonquians of New England and their old bitter enemies, the Iroquois of New York, are meeting together. Everywhere Indian people are trying to unite to solve the problems they have in common.

Thanksgiving Day, 1970, was declared "A National Day of Mourning for Native Americans." About 200 Indians from 25 tribes met at Plymouth Rock in Massachusetts. There were Cheyenne, Cherokee, Chippewa, Sioux, Mohawk, Passamaquoddy, Wampanoag, and Narragansett. They were called together by the United American Indians of New England.

While the white people were gathered to celebrate the 350-year anniversary of the landing of the Pilgrims, the Indians were there to give their view of that historic event.

They gathered at the statue of Massasoit overlooking Plymouth Rock. Some boarded *Mayflower II* standing in port and climbed its riggings. They said they were there to talk and the white man must listen! Tall Oak, a Narragansett, said, "We mourn the fact that our land is now occupied by a nation that—ignores and even rejects the people of the land." They see Plymouth Rock as a symbol of all the terrible things that have happened to them.

Indians living on or off reservations want more jobs, better education, and better medical care. They want their children to learn their own history and language and to learn about their heroes. They want discrimination to end. They ask for the return of surplus land—land no longer used by the United States government. They feel they have this right because this was arranged by treaties between Indians and the United States government many years ago. On such land they would build community centers, special schools, and housing and health centers. Indians want to be independent. They want to reestablish their rights and their power as a people.

Places to Visit

THERE ARE MANY PLACES IN NEW ENGLAND that will remind you of the early days of the Woodland Indians. Here are some of them.

In Uncasville, Connecticut, there is the Tantaquidgeon Indian Museum. Chief Tantaquidgeon who will welcome you is a Mohegan. He traces his ancestry back to Chief Sassacus and Chief Uncas.

On the grounds of the museum you will see the framework of a wigwam. You can see how the thin, spindly saplings are arched over and lashed together. Inside the museum there are slender, polished bows, arrow tips, and stone blades. You will be able to pick up a wooden war club and feel how heavy and well-balanced it is. You will see how some war clubs are shaped from one strong piece of wood and how others have ball-shaped stone heads lashed to wooden handles.

Chief Tantaquidgeon teaches groups of schoolchildren Indian stone- and woodworking crafts.

In Mystic, Connecticut, there was once the large palisaded village of the Pequot Indians that was burned to the ground in the Pequot War. Near that spot there is a statue of Captain John Mason. It is a bitter note, however, for Captain Mason was the English military commander who ordered the burning of the fort.

In Mystic there are other reminders of the Pequots—road signs that say Pequot Road, Pequot Trail.

At Ashaway, Rhode Island, there is the Tomaquag Indian Memorial Museum. Princess Red Wing is the director. She comes from Wampanoag and Narragansett ancestry. She wants American children to know the history and crafts of her people. She spends a great deal of time speaking at schools.

At the museum she shows groups of children the utensils Indians used to cook dinner and the different baskets used for storage. She also teaches children Indian dances and songs.

There is a maple sugar tree growing on the museum grounds. In early March, when the sap begins to flow, Maple Sugar Ceremonies are held. The tree is tapped with a wooden trough in the old Indian way.

In the village of Arcadia, Exeter, Rhode Island, there is a restaurant, Dovecrest, owned by Indians. You can eat Johnny cakes or Journey cakes, the modern version of Indian on-the-trail food. You can also eat Indian pudding, a delicious mixture now made of stone-ground cornmeal, spices, molasses, eggs, and milk.

Next to the restaurant is a trading post where you can see an old Indian ceremonial peace pipe called the *Calumet*. There is a large collection of arrowheads made by Narragansetts. You will see a large skinning stone once used to remove fur and fat from the skin of a freshly killed animal. There is also a huge, 200-pound stone mortar and rolling pestle once used to grind corn.

In South Kingston, Rhode Island, a large monument marks the historic site of the Great Swamp Fight in King Philip's War.

In Bristol, Rhode Island, the Haffenreffer Museum of Anthropology is built on Mount Hope. It stands on a slope overlooking the broad sweep of Mount Hope Bay. At one time Mount Hope was the summer village of Massasoit and then of his son Metacomet. Not far from that spot Metacomet was ambushed and killed in King Philip's War.

The Haffenreffer Museum has special education programs. There is a section on the Northeast Indians. Children can sit in a real wigwam around a warm fire and handle the tools of the Indian people. They can eat Indian food and learn some games and dances. There is a craft program in beadwork and featherwork.

In Massachusetts there is the Mashpee Indian Village on Cape Cod. The Mashpees hope to build a museum and restore a Wampanoag Village. They are also restoring the Old Indian Church, the oldest Indian church in America. Meantime you can visit a craft shop, "Little Indian Village," and find some interesting things.

Then you can take a ferry over to Gay Head on Vineyard Haven Island. It is a village of Indian artists. There are painters and craftsmen doing pottery and beadwork.

In Plymouth, Massachusetts, there are many places to visit. There is the fourteen-foot high bronze statue of Massasoit. It stands on Cole's Hill overlooking Plymouth Rock.

Nearby is the Plymouth National Wax Museum. In it are a few scenes showing early encounters between the Indians and the Pilgrims.

Outdoors at "Plimoth Plantation, Inc.," there is a fine example of the framework of a Wampanoag summer house. It is set in the center of the family's vegetable garden. You will see how fish are strung up on a rack of sticks to dry in the sun.

In Maine you will be welcomed at the three Indian reservations. But it is advisable to write in advance to the tribal councils and let them know you would like to visit. They welcome schoolchildren.

Often during the summer there are Indian celebrations at some of the villages and reservations. You can see Indian dances, ceremonies, and games and eat Indian food.

Each state in New England has other museums of interest.
Some of them are:

> The Peabody Museum of Natural History, Yale University, New Haven, Connecticut.
> The Children's Museum, Boston, Massachusetts.
> The Peabody Museum of Archaeology and Ethnology, Cambridge, Massachusetts.
> The Salt Pond Visitor Center in Eastham on Cape Cod, Massachusetts.

Throughout New England there are hundreds and hundreds of Indian names of mountains, roads, streams, lakes, rivers, caves, islands, and rocks. You will see some of these names when you look at the road map as you travel from place to place. These are all reminders of the people to whom the land once belonged.

Where to Write

BEFORE YOU VISIT the museums, reservations, and villages listed in this book, it is a good idea to write to them to find out the days and hours they are open to visitors. Here are the addresses.

The Tantaquidgeon Indian Museum
Uncasville, Connecticut

The Tomaquag Indian Memorial Museum
Princess Red Wing, Director
Ashaway, Rhode Island

Dovecrest Restaurant and Trading Post
Mrs. Eleanor Dove
Arcadia Village
Exeter, Rhode Island

Haffenreffer Museum of Anthropology
Mount Hope
Bristol, Rhode Island

The Mashpee Indian Council
Mashpee, Massachusetts

Plymouth National Wax Museum
Plymouth, Massachusetts

"Plimoth Plantation, Inc."
Plymouth, Massachusetts

The Tribal Council
Penobscot Indian Reservation
Indian Island, Old Town
Maine

The Tribal Council
Pleasant Point Reservation
Perry, Maine

The Tribal Council
Indian Township Reservation
Princeton, Maine

Suggested
Further Reading

Bjorklund, Karna; *The Indians of Northeastern America,* Dodd, Mead and Co., New York, 1969.

Edwards, Cecile Pepin; *King Philip—Loyal Indian,* Houghton Mifflin Co., Boston, 1962. This is historical fiction.

Elting, Mary and Folsom, Franklin; *The Story of Archaeology in America*, Harvey House, Irvington-on-Hudson, 1960.

Glubok, Shirley; *The Art of the North American Indian*, Harper and Row, New York, 1964.

Hofsinde, Robert; *Indian Games and Crafts*, William Morrow, New York, 1957.

Hofsinde, Robert; *Indian Music Makers*, William Morrow, New York, 1967.

La Farge, Oliver; *The American Indian*, special edition for young readers, Golden Press, New York, 1969.

May, Julian; *Before the Indians*, Holiday House, New York, 1969.

Rosebud Yellow Robe; *An Album of the American Indian*, Franklin Watts, Inc., New York, 1969.

Stephens, Peter John; *Towappu, Puritan Renegade*, Atheneum, New York, 1966. This is fiction.

White, Anne T.; *The American Indian*, adapted for young readers, an American Heritage Book of Indians, Random House, New York, 1963.

Wissler, Clark; *Indians of the United States*, Doubleday and Co., New York, 1956.